CITY OF ANGELS

Project Managers: Jeannette DeLisa & Sy Feldman
Art Layout: Lisa Greene Mane
Motion Picture Artwork: © 1998 Warner Bros.
All Rights Reserved

CONTENTS

UNINVITED

Words and Music by
ALANIS MORISSETTE

Uninvited - 5 - 1
PF9816

4

MAMA, YOU'VE (GOT A DAUGHTER)
(MAMA, YOU GOT A DAUGHTER)

Words and Music by
JOHN LEE HOOKER

Repeat ad lib. and fade

Rap & solo vamp

Verse 2:
Tell your daughter I love her;
I'll love her till the day I die.
Tell your daughter I love her;
I'll love her till the day I die.
I want you to talk to your daughter;
Talk to your daughter for me.

FURTHER ON UP THE ROAD

Words and Music by
JOE VEASEY and DON ROBEY

IRIS

Tune Guitar
*DADDAD

Words and Music by
JOHN RZEZNIK

*Tune 4th string down to match 3rd string D.

Iris - 11 - 1
PF9816

ANGEL

Words and Music by
SARAH McLACHLAN

Em7 / Fm7

si - lent____ rev - er - ie.____ You're in the

F / Gb   Fsus / Gbsus   F / Gb

arms of____ the an - gel where you

C / Db   Am7 / Bbm7   G7 / Ab

1.

find_____ some com - fort____

C / Db   F/C / Gb/Db

____ here.____

some com - fort_____ here._____

I KNOW

Words and Music by
MICHAEL JUDE CHRISTODAL

Slow alternative rock style ♩.= 50

Verse:

1. You've got_____ such a_____
2. *See additional lyrics*

___ pret - ty smile._____

It's a shame, the

the feel - ing____ of "a - lone."

I know____

that you do not____ feel in - vit - ed.____

But come____ back,

42

Verse 2:
Step away then, from the edge.
Your best friend in life is not your mirror.
Back away, come back away, come back away,
Come back away, come back away, come back away.
I am here, and I will be, forever and ever.
And I....
(To Chorus 2:)

Chorus 2:
I know there's nowhere you can hide it.
I know the feeling of alone.
Trust me, and don't keep that on the inside.
Soon you, you'll be locked out on your own.

CITY OF ANGELS

By
GABRIEL YARED

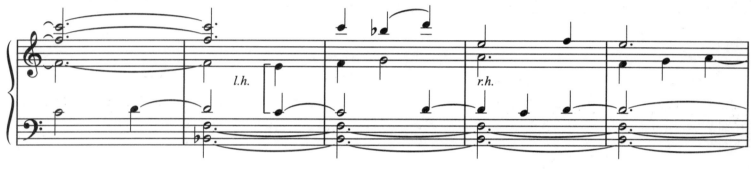

City of Angels - 6 - 1
PF9816

A little faster (♩ = 80)

mf

Slowly (♩ = 63)

FEELIN' LOVE

Words and Music by
PAULA COLE

54

Am I____ Bar - ry____ White, am____ I Is - is?____

Lov - er,____ I'm laced____ with your____ un - con -

scious._____ I will____ be your__

__ Des - de - mo - na._____

Verse 2:
You make me feel like a candy apple, all red and horny.
You make me feel like I want to be dumb blonde
In a centerfold; the girl next door.
And I would open the door and I'd be all wet,
With my tits soaking through this tiny little T-shirt
That I'm wearing and you would open the door
And tie me up to the bed.
(To Chorus:)

THE UNFEELING KISS

By
GABRIEL YARED

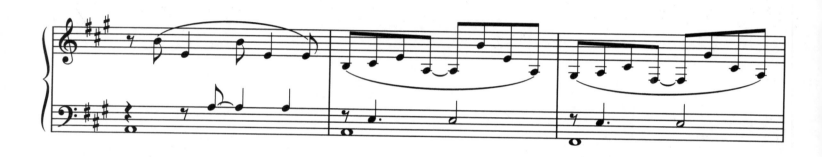

The Unfeeling Kiss - 6 - 1
PF9816

Slowly (♩ = 80)
"An Angel Falls"

Slower (♩ = 70)

"The Unfeeling Kiss"

pp

sub. *p*

dim.

IF GOD WILL SEND HIS ANGELS

Music by
U2

Lyrics by
BONO and THE EDGE

and if God___ would send___ his___ an - gels, would- ev - 'ry- thing be___

___ al - right?

% *Verses 2-4:*

2. God has got his phone___ off the hook, babe, would - n't e - ven
moth - er deal - in' in___ a door - way. See Fa - ther
4. Je - sus nev - er let me down, you know, Je - sus

Repeat ad lib. and fade